The Definitive Guide to Ace Your Interview and Get the Job

By
Vijay Ingam, CFA

The Definitive Guide to Ace Your Interview and Get the Job

Contents

Guide Contents 3

About Interview Sos 4

Suggested Preparation Time For An Interview 5

Suggestions For The Interview 6

What Do You Bring And Wear To A Job Interview? 8

Research And Preparation Prior To The Interview 12

Guidelines For Answering Job Interview Questions 15

The Most Common Job Interview Questions 20

Telephone Interviews 30

Panel Interviews 32

How To Prepare For Skills Testing 34

Thank You Notes 37

Conclusion 39

Guide Contents

This short guide is designed to help a job applicant like you prepare for an interview. It will advise you on:

- What to bring and wear to an interview
- How to research the company prior to your interview
- What aspects of your background to emphasize during the interview
- How to answer the most common job interview questions
- How to avoid pitfalls in the process
- How to deal with a telephone interview or a panel interview
- How to write a thank you note after the interview
- How to accept a job offer

This guide is comprehensive but concise. It's designed to tell you all the basic information you need to know to succeed in your interview. If you have additional questions or concerns, consult an Interview SOS career coach.

About Interview SOS

We hope you'll consider using Interview SOS career services as part of your successful job search. Interview SOS provides the following career services:

- Resume writing
- Job interview preparation
- Graduate school interview preparation
- Career counseling services

We meet with clients across the USA and around the world using the telephone, Skype, and Google Chat. Our company is led by experienced career services professionals who are committed to providing top notch career coaching to our clients. Our headquarters is in Los Angeles, California. This book is written by Vijay Ingam, the founder of Interview SOS.

Call us at 1-800-212-2670 or the visit the Interview SOS website at **www.interviewsos.com** to find out more.

Suggested Preparation Time for an Interview

You should expect to spend 2-8 hours preparing for a typical job interview. **The more time you spend preparing for a job interview, the more likely you are to get the job.** Remember that your overall goal in the job interview process is to impress the hiring manager(s) enough to pick you over the other applicants by presenting your educational background, skills, credentials, work experience and personality in the best possible light. If you come to an interview having completed the preparations described in this guide, you should be better prepared than the vast majority of job applicants; that's how you get the job. Candidates with special situations or those applying for specific job types may require additional preparation. Consult your interview coach for guidance.

Suggestions for the Interview

- Always be 30 minutes early for a job interview and plan to have reliable transportation ahead of time.

- Start your conversation with each interviewer by greeting them with a firm handshake.

- Dress in business formal attire (see our guidelines below).

- Express your interest in the company very early in the interview. You can say, "I am very excited to have the opportunity to interview for this position."

- Maintain eye contact with your interviewer and smile.

- Ask each interviewer to give you a business card or professional contact info, including email (you will need this to send a thank you note and in order to follow up later).

- Be friendly and conversational with everyone you encounter, including administrative staff, other candidates for the position, and security

Plan to be 30 minutes early to your job interview.

What Do You Bring and Wear to a Job Interview?

We have the following suggestions regarding attire and personal grooming for men and women during job interviews.

Recommended Attire for Men

- A recently dry cleaned and pressed navy blue, grey, or black suit
- A blue or white collared button-down long sleeve shirt (pinstripes are acceptable)
- A nice but conservative tie
- Dark colored socks
- Brown or black leather belt and shoes
- No sandals or open-toed shoes
- Conservatively combed hair (if you have long hair, put it in a ponytail)
- The only jewelry you should wear is a wristwatch
- Pull out your earring if you have one (you

can wear it later, just not during the interview)

Recommended Attire for Women

- ➢ A recently dry cleaned and pressed dark blue, black, cream, beige, or grey dress suit (make sure the length is below the knees) or pantsuit

- ➢ Conservative leather shoes (no open-toed shoes)

- ➢ Hair in a bun, ponytail, or in a carefully-combed conservative hairstyle

- ➢ Limited jewelry and tastefully done makeup

Appropriate Attire for a Job Interview

For both sexes we suggest:

- ➢ Shower well, groom yourself, and rinse with mouthwash or use breath mints before the interview.

- ➢ Conceal any tattoos.

These guidelines are applicable in the vast majority of interview situations. Please consult your interview coach if you need any clarification.

We suggest that you bring the following items to your interview:

- ➢ Two copies of your resume on white resume paper

- ➢ A list of references (call your references to confirm they are prepared to answer inquiries) or letters of recommendation

- ➢ A complete work and salary history including dates of employment, location, salary, and contact information for all prior employers

- ➢ Copies of any professional certifications

- ➢ A leather portfolio with a notepad

- ➢ Two pens (black or blue)

- ➢ Your cellular phone (turned off before the interview begins)
- ➢ A copy of your driver's license, social security card, and passport

Having these items on hand will facilitate your application process and aid you in completing any required paperwork.

Grooming and hygiene are always important for an interview.

Research and Preparation Prior to the Interview

You should anticipate spending 2-8 hours researching the job, the company, and preparing answers to interview questions prior to a typical job interview. If you know the company or the industry well, you may require less time.

Research the company and your role in it

Read the job description

- ➢ Identify the key skills and traits required for the position.

- ➢ Identify aspects of your background (education, job history, interests, etc.) that show you have those skills and traits. Make a list and try to touch upon these during the job interview.

Research the company

- ➢ Read the company website and recent press releases.

- ➢ Google the company, along with the business

unit you will be working in.

- ➢ Know the basic facts about the company, such as how large they are, where they have offices, and the nature of their main business.

- ➢ Research how your role fits into the company.

- ➢ If you can learn about the people who will be interviewing you, research their backgrounds as well.

- ➢ Reach out to any contacts you have in the organization; tell them you will be interviewing for a job and ask them for feedback and advice.

Prepare 4-8 questions for the interviewer

- ➢ These questions should subtly show that you researched the company and think positively about it. Examples:

    - "I noticed you recently hired a new CEO, Person X, do you expect positive changes in the company's business as a result?"

    - "On your website you describe your exciting new product Z, how are customers responding to this product?"

➢ You can always ask your interviewer questions about their personal experience at the company. Examples:

- "How long have you been at company X?"
- "What has your experience at company X been like?"

The best prepared job applicant usually gets the job.

Guidelines for Answering Job Interview Questions

What Employers Are Looking For

Before you begin preparing answers to common job interview questions, you need to know the characteristics that employers are looking for in potential applicants. Employers typically like job applicants with the following traits:

- Reliable
- Proactive and take initiative
- Work well in teams
- Have energy and enthusiasm
- Self-motivated
- Versatile
- Organized

Throughout the job interview, try to subtly show you have the above characteristics by providing examples from your professional or academic experience in which you demonstrated these traits.

Motivations, Aspirations, and Thought Process

The biggest mistake that most job applicants make is not presenting their motivations, aspirations, and internal thought processes in a positive light. Some examples of common mistakes:

- ➢ Don't say you quit your job because you disliked your boss, instead, say you did it because you felt there was no room to grow or you were interested in another opportunity, etc.

- ➢ Don't say you're interested in a position because of the money; say you're interested in the growth opportunities or your admiration for the company, etc.

Acceptable motivations include interest in the job and the industry, a desire to expand your knowledge and skills, or seeking greater challenges. Your thoughts are your own, so always present your internal thought process in a positive light.

Prepare your answers to common job interview questions before the interview.

You'll want to follow these guidelines in answering interview questions:

- ➢ Make sure your answers are clear and easy to understand (as a guideline, your answer should be simple enough that a high school senior could understand it).

- ➢ Focus on fulfilling the needs of the company that is hiring you, not your own needs.

- ➢ Prepare your answers to common job interview questions before your interview and rehearse your answers.

- Show you have the required skills described in the job description.

- Prove you can handle yourself professionally in the workforce and will be a reliable employee.

- Show you have insight into the importance of your work and its impact on your previous employers.

- Whenever possible, mention the positive financial impact of your activities ("saved $100K annually" or "led to $300K in additional revenue").

- Provide examples of yourself proactively seeking solutions to workplace problems.

- Never repeat a negative assessment of your performance made by someone else.

- Never say anything bad about a past employer, coworker, boss, teacher, or anyone else during a job interview.

- Never swear.

- You can sugar coat the truth, but never lie during a job interview.

The Definitive Guide to Ace Your Interview and Get the Job

A firm handshake and a winning smile can get you the job.

The Most Common Job Interview Questions

Question 1: "Tell me about yourself."

Give a short 2-3 minute pitch summarizing your background, credentials, and skills as related to the job you are applying for. This is often called an "elevator pitch." Focus on your personal, professional, and academic achievements. There are many ways to answer this question; we suggest starting with your professional goals and current position. Next, go through your resume in chronological order, including jobs and education. Summarize each job or aspect of your educational background in 1-3 sentences, focusing on your accomplishments. End by saying how your experience and background make you the ideal candidate for this position.

Current Job or Profession

Example: "I'm an experienced financial analyst"

Aspiration or Professional Goal (should be related to the job you are applying for)

Example: "Seeking a role as the Director of Finance in your company."

Education: Institutions studied at, degrees pursued including notable, career-relevant achievements, or activities at each institution

Example: "I got my BA in Accounting from USC, where I was president of my sorority Kappa Zeta and took coursework in financial modeling."

Work History: Mention past jobs, including company name, your role, the number of years you worked there, and major accomplishments, achievements, and recognition.

Example: "After graduating, I worked as an accountant at Bank of X for 5 years, during which I was promoted from junior accountant to manager. My major accomplishments included landing 3 new accounts for the company totaling $3 m in new revenue and streamlining our accounting system resulting in $100 k in annual cost savings. I currently manage 3 junior analysts."

Mention Credentials:

Example: "I have completed the requirements for the CPA designation, and I am licensed in the state of California."

Summary: End by summarizing how your skills, educational background, and work experience will make you an ideal candidate for the position described.

Example: "In summation, I think that my educational background in accounting and work experience in finance have made me into a proactive, detail-oriented financial manager who is a good fit for this role."

Complete Example:

I'm an experienced financial analyst, seeking a role as the Director of Finance in your company. I got my BA in Accounting from USC, where I was president of my sorority Kappa Zeta and took coursework in financial modeling. After graduating, I worked as an accountant at Bank of X for 5 years, during which I was promoted from junior accountant to manager. My major accomplishments included landing 3 new accounts for the company totaling $3 m in new revenue and streamlining our accounting system resulting in $100 k in annual cost savings. I currently manage 3 junior analysts. I have completed the requirements for the CPA designation, and I am licensed in the state of California. In summation, I think that my educational background in accounting and work experience in finance have made me into a proactive, detail-oriented financial manager who is a good fit for this role."

After going through the major items in your resume, you'll have to trim or add content in your elevator pitch to fit into the 2-3 minute timeframe. Always try to focus on the most important career relevant portions of your resume when writing the elevator pitch.

Make sure you ask for feedback about your elevator pitch from your Interview SOS career coach (or a friend). Practice your pitch until it comes naturally to you.

Interview SOS career coaches really add value when providing feedback on your answers to common job interview questions.

Question 2: Why are you leaving your current job, or why did you leave your previous job?

When answering this question, always focus on the positive. Mention the things you will gain from the new position, such as added responsibility or new opportunities, rather than negative aspects of your current or last job. You should never criticize your current employer or the people you work with. Don't mention salary as a primary motivator.

Question 3: What is your greatest strength? What are your strengths?

Select strengths that are appropriate for the job. Cite examples from your work experience or education that demonstrate you have that strength.

Question 4: What is your greatest weakness? What are your weaknesses?

This question is important for showing self-insight as part of the job interview process. Don't say that you have no weaknesses. Instead, focus on:

- ➢ Weaknesses you have corrected
- ➢ Strengths that are weaknesses in specific situations

Question 5: Why are you interested in this position or company?

This question is an opportunity for you to demonstrate your research regarding the company. You should say that you are interested in the company or job because of growth opportunities, your admiration for the company's products or mission, or other aspects of the job that align with your personal goals and ambitions. Don't say your primary motivator is salary.

Question 6: Tell me about your greatest achievement.

It's better to use a work-related success to answer this question, but you can also use examples from your educational background. The situation-action-result framework is useful in answering questions like this one. You should identify the situation and problems that you encountered (situation), how you overcame them (action), and the positive consequences of your efforts, preferably financial (results).

Example:

"My greatest achievement is the turnaround plan I wrote for the underperforming smaller stores of company Y."

Situation

"Company Y had underperforming small stores that were about the size of Radio Shack, and they were run as if they were larger stores the size of Best Buy."

Action

"After speaking to the store's staff and analyzing their financial statements, I began to realize the smaller stores were underperforming due to excess inventory, inefficiently scheduled staff, and lack of locally targeted marketing. I came up with a comprehensive turnaround plan that included reducing inventory, adjusting staff scheduling, and targeting marketing expenditures to local markets."

Result

"The company saved $500 k in reduced inventory and witnessed an increase in sales of 30% or about $1 million a year. Making these smaller stores work was critical for the potential future growth of the company in smaller markets."

The situation-action-result framework can also be used to answer other job interview questions.

Question 7: How do you deal with conflict?

The appropriate answer to this question is to say that you are a "peacemaker" or a "mediator" who tries to resolve workplace conflicts, while enabling those with conflicting personalities to work together. Provide a specific example of a situation at work or at school in which people found themselves at odds but were nevertheless able to overcome their differences and work together. Mention specific things you did to overcome conflicts.

Never say or imply that you often find yourself in conflict with other people (regardless of who is to blame).

The Definitive Guide to Ace Your Interview and Get the Job

How do you plan to respond to discrimination if you encounter it?

Dealing with Illegal Questions

In the United States, it's generally illegal to ask job interview questions regarding:

- ➢ Race
- ➢ Religion
- ➢ Ethnic background
- ➢ Sexual orientation
- ➢ Children
- ➢ Marital status

> Age

However, we live in the real world, where companies and interviewers are not aware of the law and sometimes discriminate. We suggest that you use your own judgment in answering these types of questions should they come up. You may no longer be interested in working for the company after being asked a discriminatory question.

Our suggested response to an illegal question is:

"I'm sorry, but I don't feel it's appropriate for me to answer that question as part of my job interview. However, I would be happy to discuss how my skills and qualifications make me the best candidate for this job."

Telephone Interviews

Companies often use telephone interviews to screen job applicants before bringing them into further rounds of interviewing. Telephone interviews can also be used if a hiring manager is in a remote location. Telephone interviews should be viewed just as seriously as in person interviews. Similar preparations are required. The primary difficulty with telephone interviews is that it can be hard to respond to questions given over the phone because you don't have the visual cues from facial expressions and body language to assess your interviewer's thinking. However, there are also some advantages to telephone interviews. For instance, you can easily refer to your notes during a telephone interview. We suggest you take advantage of this benefit by having your notes handy during the interview (Don't read straight from your notes.).

Our recommendations for telephone interviews include:

> Prepare as if it was a regular interview.

> Sit alone at a table in a quiet room with your interview preparation notes handy during the interview.

> Make hand gestures and speak as if your interviewer were in front of you.

> Make sure you have a reliable phone, preferably a landline, ready for the interview. If you have to use a cellular phone, make sure it is completely charged and has excellent reception prior to the interview.

> Remember that your tone of voice is particularly important in a telephone interview, because that's how you convey your enthusiasm and feelings.

You can refer to your notes during a telephone interview.

Panel Interviews

Sometimes you'll face a team of interviewers instead of a single interviewer. The panel interview requires that you connect with all of these interviewers at the same time. Expect to get questions from all of the panel members at some point during the interview. Our suggestions for panel interviews include:

> Prepare as it if was a regular interview.

> Move down the line of interviewers and make sure you introduce yourself to each one with a firm handshake and a smile at the beginning of the interview.

> When you answer a question from a specific panel member, start by having eye contact with the panel member asking the question, and after about 20 seconds, adjust your eye contact to address other members of the group to show you are directing your answer to them as well.

> Ask for a business card from every member of the panel and send a unique thank you note to each.

Don't be afraid of panel interviews!

How to Prepare for Skills Testing

Sometimes employers will give you skills tests to assess your knowledge of the software programs you'll be using, along with other tests concerning skills or knowledge required for the position. They will usually warn you ahead of time so you can be prepared for such testing. Sometimes an employer will use testing software that is designed to assess your skills and knowledge. Other times they will ask you to demonstrate your ability to perform a few common functions on a computer program or answer a few questions about a specific subject. The best way to prepare for a skills test is to know the subject or computer program you are being tested on, but be aware that sometimes skills tests can be on aspects of a subject or computer program that you do not use regularly. Interview SOS suggests the following preparations:

Tests on Microsoft Office Applications (Microsoft Excel, Word, PowerPoint, Access or Outlook)

Before taking a skills test on a Microsoft Office program, we suggest you use the **Professor Teaches Office 2010** from Individual Software. It's a great program that shows you how to use most basic functions on each of the major programs of the Microsoft Office Suite. Expect to spend 3-4 hours learning the basic functions for each program. We suggest doing both the basic and advanced lessons for each office program prior to a skills test.

Typing Tests

We suggest using either **Mavis Beacon Teaches Typing** or **Typing Instructor** before taking a test to improve your typing skills. Depending on your current typing skills and those required for the position, you should anticipate spending 10-40 hours learning to type well if you don't have the skill already.

Accounting Software

To prepare for tests on accounting software such as Sage Peachtree, we suggest using **Mastering Peachtree Made Easy Training Tutorial**. To learn QuickBooks, we suggest **Mastering QuickBooks Made Easy v. 2013 Video Training Tutorial Course DVD-ROM**.

Subject Tests

If you anticipate a subject test on something like financial accounting or nursing, we suggest spending a few hours reviewing a respected textbook on the subject, even if you feel you are already knowledgeable.

Thank You Notes

Write a thank you note after the interview (be sure to get a business card from the hiring manager). The thank you note does the following:

- ➢ Shows your appreciation to the interviewer for taking the time to meet with you.

- ➢ Expresses your continued interest in the job.

- ➢ Mentions something professionally-related about the job interview you found interesting (always positive).

- ➢ Reminds the interviewer about any aspects of your background that make you especially qualified for the position.

- ➢ Should be sent within 24 hours! Email is best, but written notes are acceptable if mailed the same day.

- ➢ Send a unique note to each person you interviewed with.

Sample thank you note

Dear [Person X],

The Definitive Guide to Ace Your Interview and Get the Job

Thank you for taking the time to meet with me to discuss my interest in [position A] at [company Z]. I particularly enjoyed our discussion regarding _____.

I was very excited about the position because of _____.

I think I'm a good candidate because _____.

Thanks,

[Your name]

Conclusion

Thank you for reading this guide. We hope you will consider using our services as part of your successful job search. Call us at 1-800-212-2670 or the visit the Interview SOS website at **www.interviewsos.com** to find out more.

Good luck on your interview!

Interview SOS – Our Mission

Our mission is to provide an educational service that helps job applicants succeed in the interview process by demonstrating their skills, experience, and educational credentials. The interview is the most critical piece of the job application process, and we want our clients to be able to present themselves in the best possible way. We help our clients by giving them an assessment of their applications and helping them to emphasize their strengths and mitigate weaknesses. We want our clients to feel confident, well prepared, and aware of what to expect during the job interview.

About Vijay Ingam

Vijay is an experienced financial analyst, career coach and hiring manager, who was disappointed with the interview skills of many job applicants, even those from top-ranked business schools. In 2009, Vijay began offering personalized interview coaching and resume writing services in Los Angeles. He subsequently founded Interview SOS.

Vijay was a student career coach for the Parker Career Management Center (UCLA Anderson School of Management's MBA-level career counseling service) and a Boston-area diversity recruiter and interviewer for the Sponsors for Educational Opportunity Career Program. Vijay's past employers include Citibank, US Bank, State Street Corporation, the McGraw-Hill Companies, and Bain Capital-owned Guitar Center.

Vijay has an undergraduate degree in Economics from the University of Chicago and an MBA from the UCLA Anderson School of Management in Los Angeles, California. He is a National Merit Scholar and CFA charter holder. Vijay also has experience in healthcare, having passed the USMLE

Step 1 and attending medical school for 2 years.

Vijay's sister, Mindy Kaling, is the executive producer, writer, and star of the *Mindy Project* on Fox Television.

www.ingramcontent.com/pod-product-compliance
Lightning Source LLC
Chambersburg PA
CBHW071548170526
45166CB00004B/1594